edward de bono's
mind
power

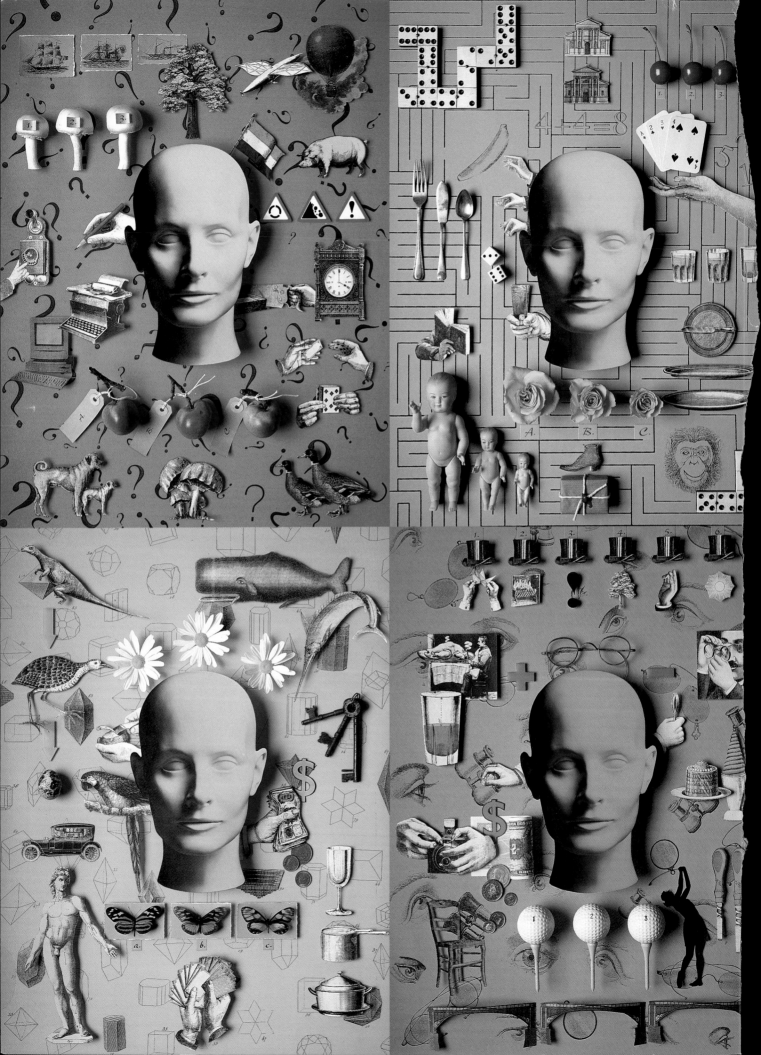

edward de bono's
mind
power

DORLING KINDERSLEY

LONDON • NEW YORK • STUTTGART • MOSCOW

A DORLING KINDERSLEY BOOK

Art editor	Mark Johnson Davies
Editor	Neil Lockley
US editor	Laaren Brown
DTP designer	Zirrinia Austin
Assistant designer	Stephen Croucher
Project editor	Louise Candlish
Managing editor	Sean Moore
Production controller	Meryl Silbert
Picture research	Lorna Ainger
DK Picture Library	Caroline Potts

First American Edition, 1995

2 4 6 8 10 9 7 5 3 1

Published in the United States by Dorling Kindersley Publishing, Inc.
95 Madison Avenue, New York, New York 10016

Published in Great Britain by Dorling Kindersley Limited.

Distributed by Houghton Mifflin Company, Boston.

Library of Congress Cataloging-in-Publication Data

De Bono, Edward, 1933-
    Mind power / by Edward De Bono.
        p.   cm.
    ISBN 1-56458-864-5
    1. Human information processing.   2. Creative thinking.
3. Thought and thinking.   I. Title.
BF444.D43 1995
153.4--dc20
                                                        95-19318
                                                        CIP

Color reproduction by Colourscan, Singapore

Manufactured in China by Imago

contents

how to enjoy thinking

Your brain is the MOST
IMPORTANT thing you have.

*Then why don't you enjoy
using it?* Because thinking
is *hard work* and *serious,*
and even BORING.

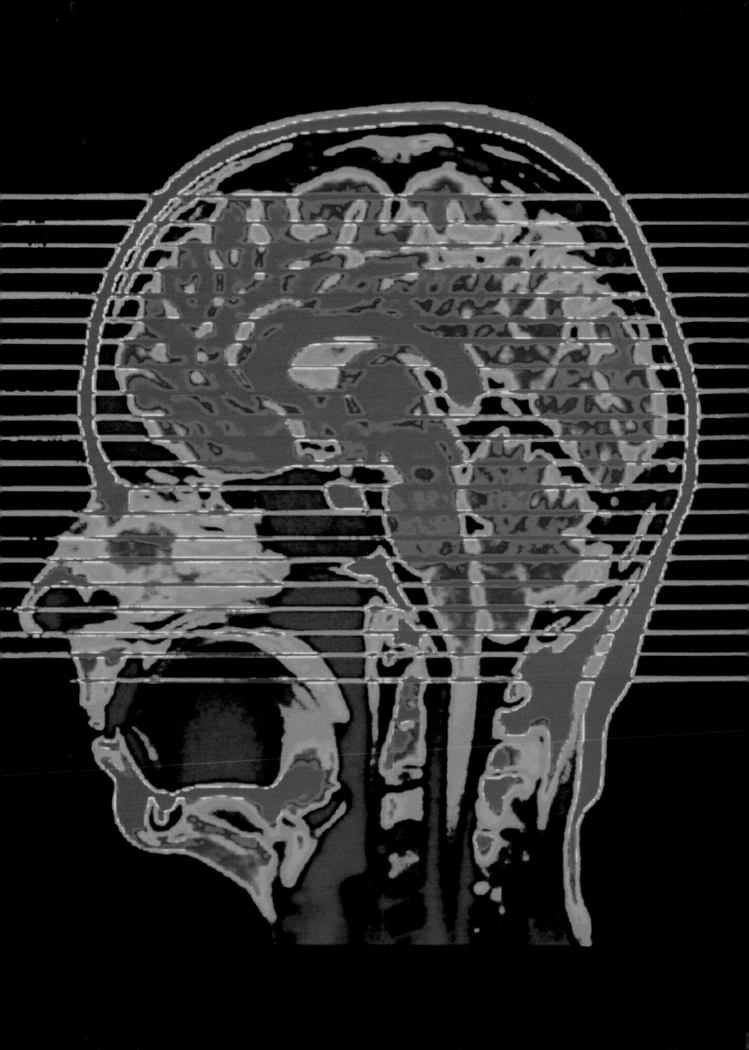

How many hours a week do you spend watching television? Twenty? Twenty-five? Thirty? And how many hours listening to music? And how many hours actively using your brain? Watching television is very enjoyable, but passive. Listening to music may exercise your feelings, but not your brain.

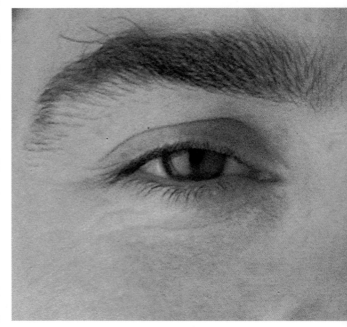

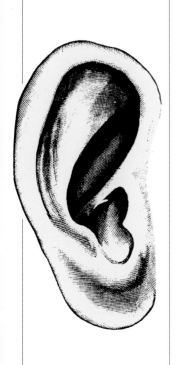

Some people believe that thinking is just a matter of intelligence. They assume that if you are born with a high IQ, then you can think, and if not, then it is just too bad. This is complete nonsense. In my experience, many highly intelligent people are bad thinkers. They know how to defend their point of view, but that is all. Many people with a lower IQ are much better thinkers.

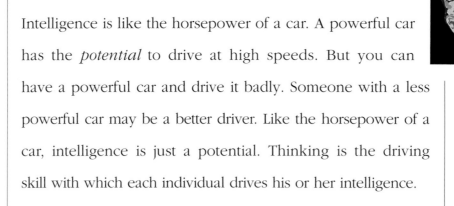

Intelligence is like the horsepower of a car. A powerful car has the *potential* to drive at high speeds. But you can have a powerful car and drive it badly. Someone with a less powerful car may be a better driver. Like the horsepower of a car, intelligence is just a potential. Thinking is the driving skill with which each individual drives his or her intelligence.

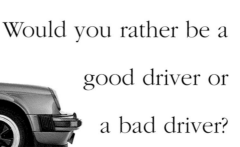

Would you rather be a good driver or a bad driver?

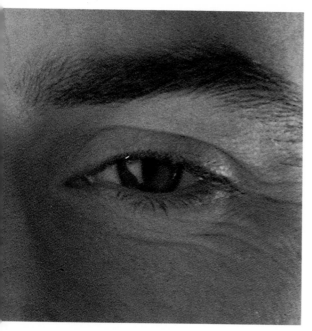

Anyone can develop a high degree of skill in thinking if he or she wants to do so. That means making some effort. That is the purpose of this book: to make it easy to develop your personal skill in thinking. There is no point in expecting schools, or even universities, to develop your thinking skill for you. In my experience, very few do. Even when thinking is taught, this is usually of the analytical and critical type. This is useful, but it is only one part of thinking.

So it is up to you.

Thinking is not a matter of getting the right answer. It is a matter of consciously using your mind, and enjoying using it. Treat thinking like a sport. Have fun. In sports, training may be boring at times, but you know you are getting better all the time as you train.

Why bother to learn thinking? Why not just pick it up as you go along? Because *the sort of thinking you will just pick up may be very limited.* In any sport, coaching makes a big difference.

IT IS THE SAME WITH THINKING.

This book covers some of the basic aspects of thinking. There is "perception." How do we choose to look at the world? There is the "power of possibilities." This is what has been behind the success of Western civilization in science and technology. There is the generation of "alternatives" that give us more freedom of action. There is "choice and decision," because we may sometimes have to choose between alternatives. "Judgment" is important, and so is "analysis." Then there are "values and feelings." All these things, and more, are part of the skill of thinking.

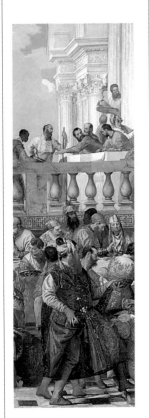

In this book you can read a little bit about these aspects of thinking. But, more importantly, you can get to practice each aspect of thinking with exercises and games that have been devised especially for this book. They have also been designed to be fun and enjoyable and to be repeated again and again.

You should not feel that you always have to get things right or always have to win at the games. You try, and you enjoy trying, and by trying you improve. You do not give up tennis because every first serve does not work. In time, more and more of your first serves will succeed.

It is the fun of thinking that matters most – not the result. Watch yourself thinking.

For the young, as you become a more and more skilled thinker you will find that this has a powerful effect on your schoolwork and examinations. In later life, skilled thinking

will be of use in personal matters and also in work matters. A thinker can take initiatives instead of waiting to be told what to do. A thinker can generate useful alternatives and make decisions. A thinker can solve problems and design ways forward.

Go through the book slowly and carefully, and try out the exercises. Knowing and doing are two different things. You can know all about a sport such as tennis, but you will only become a tennis player when you begin to practice playing the game.

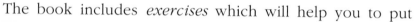

The book includes *exercises* which will help you to put your thinking skills into practice. Some of the exercises can be done on your own, but many are more fun if done with a friend, or with a group. The *games* require another player. It could be someone in your family, or a friend. Make it a joint venture with a friend to develop your thinking skills together. Adapt the rules of the games to suit your needs. Don't just play the games once. Repeat them and repeat them and watch your thinking skills improve.

Make THINKING your HOBBY!

recognition

You get home by following the road you know.

You get through life by

dealing with the things you know.

It would be useful if everything

were LABELED.

APPLE

SHIP

FLY

KETTLE

In fact, most things *are* labeled, but the labels are supplied in our minds. You write your own labels. Once the label is in place, you know what to do with that thing. You *eat* ice cream. You use a bus *to travel.*

When you take an apple out of a box labeled "apples," then you expect that apple to *taste* just as apples should taste. Once the label is clearly attached to the box, then you know immediately what you are getting out of the box. You do not need to recognize the thing all over again. You just trust the label on the box. You could sit in the dark and eat apples out of a box labeled "apples" without any surprises.

Just as our minds put LABELS on all the things with which we are familiar, so our minds put all the things with the *same label into the same box.*

COMMENT

Most of us are skilled in decoding clues – you can read the word "clues" opposite without complete letters, and you can recognize objects from their silhouettes. The 30 Questions game helps you *look* for clues where there is *nothing* to see.

This is a very powerful system. When we recognize something, we put it into a familiar labeled box. Then we remember the "instructions" on that box and we know what we should do with that thing. We have either written the instructions ourselves, or we have borrowed them from someone else. All of this helps make life extremely orderly and convenient, and much, much easier.

The easy part is getting something out of a labeled box. The more difficult part is knowing which box to put something into. Does it go here or does it go there? You come across what looks like a mushroom. Is it something that is good to eat, or is it poisonous?

It is possible that we might be able to make a guess at what something is. However, if the item in question is completely unfamiliar to us, then we can only wait until we can borrow the label and the instructions from someone else.

A

B

C

D

CAN YOU GUESS WHICH of the four types of mushrooms shown here are edible and which are poisonous? Check your answers on pages 70-71 ☞

One player shuffles the cards, then looks at the top card. No one else can see this card. The other player(s) must then discover what the card shows by asking up to 30 questions. Any question that requires only a "yes" ▶

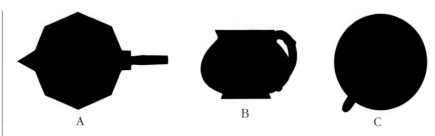

A   B   C

HOW QUICKLY can you identify these three items simply by glancing at their silhouettes? Check your answers on pages 70-71 ☞

There are times when something is very familiar but we cannot get a good look at it. So we have to carry out the recognition from parts of the whole picture. We call these

CLUES

▶ *or "no" answer counts as one question. A question that requires a fuller answer (for example, "Where is this used?") counts as five questions. A guess question counts as three questions.*

If the object remains undiscovered, the player answering the questions wins. Otherwise, the person making the winning guess is the winner. The game continues with another player taking over and drawing a card.

A

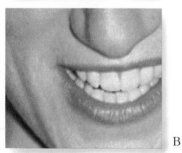

B

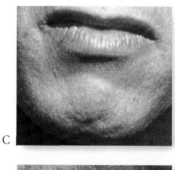

C

D

THESE PICTURES show sections of some very familiar faces. Can you recognize the faces? Check your answers on pages 70-71 ☞

THINKARD GAME

40 QUESTIONS: THE MIXED-UP THINKARD GAME

This game is very similar to the 30 Questions game (see page 15.) The procedure and scoring are exactly the same, but this time the game is much harder. Two cards ▶

THESE IMAGES ARE pieces of a painting. What do you think

is happening? For the complete picture, see pages 70-71 ☞

are drawn, and the person holding the cards has to answer for both cards, but without saying which is which.

The answers might go as follows: "Yes, for one of them"; "No, for both of them"; "One of them can be used in the…"

The questioners have to figure out one or both of the items. Because this game is more difficult than the 30 Questions game, 40 questions are allowed.

Sometimes the clues are all present but they are not together and they are all mixed up. This makes it much more difficult to recognize something.

Sometimes, we cannot actually see the object but are only told about it. We have to put the verbal clues together. Often, clues are not given and we have to ask for them. This might be what a detective does. A scientist also has to ask for clues by doing experiments.

Sometimes, when we cannot get as close a look as we would like, it is difficult to recognize things that we know well. But if we are not certain about something, or do not know it, then the closest of looks may be of no use.

COMMENT

You will find as you play the 30 and 40 Questions games that you learn to devise questions that draw out the relevant clues.

This system of recognizing something and then putting it into a box in our minds has a lot of advantages. It makes life simpler. All you have to do is to recognize something, and then you know what to do about it.

But there are also a lot of dangers that can arise from this system. The boxes may be very simple and crude, and so we will be forced to see the world in this crude and simple way. For instance, if you just had two boxes labeled

then you would have to put everyone you knew into one of these two boxes. So you would be treating as friends people who were not really your friends. And you would be treating as enemies people who were not your enemies at all.

Another danger of this system is that boxes are always based on the past. They are, therefore, not very good at dealing with the future. For example, early computers were extremely complicated to use. So someone who had only used early computers might well feel that all computers were complicated to use.

On certain occasions, we may also create labeled boxes based on limited experience. For instance, if a red-haired person bullied you at school, you might think that all red-haired people were bullies. The more boxes that you manage to develop, the more effective and useful your actions will be.

A

B

CAN YOU

IDENTIFY the eight flags shown here?

C

D

COMMENT

———

Unless you already have the labels, you will find it difficult to put a name to the flags.

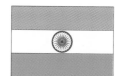

E

F

Check your answers on pages 70-71

G

H

COMMENT

———

Once you have checked the answers, you will have "borrowed" labels.

concepts

Our minds are experienced in

RECOGNIZING and LINKING two items

that are "*similar.*"

| TYPEWRITER | CAKE | CAR | HEN |
| HORSE | PENCIL | SNAKE | PAINT |

CAN YOU ARRANGE the eight items shown above into four pairs? Each pair must share a concept. Check possible answers on pages 70-71 👉

Check possible answers on pages 70-71

COMMENT

There are no "right" answers to the concept exercise above. The answers on pages 70-71 are just a few possible sets of pairs. Yours may be different, but will be just as "right."

As soon as we are asked to put items into pairs, we look for something that two items have in common. In the above exercise, a typewriter is very different from a pencil and would never go into a box labeled "pencils." Yet both pencils and typewriters are writing devices. This is a "concept" that links them together. We might have a group of items that includes chalk, pencil, typewriter, computer, marker, ballpoint pen, and fountain pen.

COMMENT

When you have made your pairings, try to make four new ones. Then try to find a concept that links each of the four items in the top row with the item beneath it.

Objects that appear quite *different* at first can often be *connected* by a COMMON CONCEPT.

STUDY CAREFULLY THE ITEMS featured below. As you can see, there are eight distinct and separate items. Can you divide the featured items into two clearly differentiated groups, each numbering four items? Use any basis that you like to create the two groups. Pause and do your own thinking before you read further.

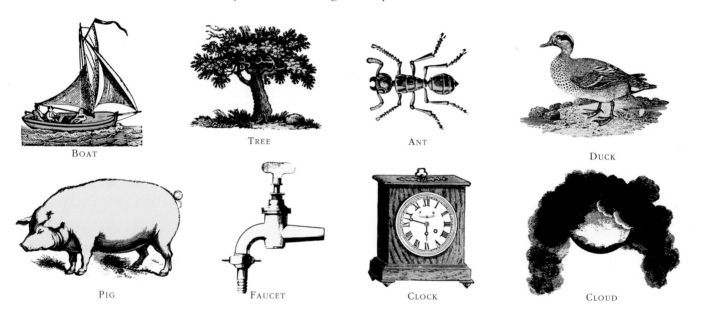

BOAT   TREE   ANT   DUCK

PIG   FAUCET   CLOCK   CLOUD

In the above grouping exercise, you might have decided that boat, tree, and clock can be grouped together on the basis that they all have (or can have) some wood in them. You might have decided that the duck, the pig, and the ant are all animals and the others are not. But that is only three items. Thinking more, you might decide that duck, cloud, boat, and faucet are all connected with water.

These are just some of the possible groupings that you might have thought of. You might have decided on your grouping on a totally different basis.

COMMENT

Once you have made your groupings, try to find *another* concept that links each group of four. Later, try to find concepts that link five, six, seven, or all eight items.

*This game is for two
players. The pack is
divided into two and
each player is dealt
half of the pack. This
is facing down.*

*Each player now turns
over the top card at
exactly the same
moment. This must
be done by turning
the card outward
(if the card were
turned inward, the
person turning it
would see it before the
other player). When
the cards are visible,
a player says "snap"* ▶

It can be easy to group items
on the basis of a *broad concept.*
It is more difficult to recognize the
NARROWER CONCEPTS involved.

THESE FOUR TYPES OF ships are linked by the broad concept that they
each move forward through water. What are the narrower concepts
involved? Pause and do your own thinking before reading further.

SAILBOAT   PADDLE STEAMER

PROPELLER SHIP   HOVERCRAFT

In the above exercise, there is a similarity between the
propeller ship and the paddle steamer. In both cases, there
is some surface pushing against the water. In both cases, the
energy is provided by an engine, in one case driving a screw
propeller, and in the other, driving a paddle wheel.

The hovercraft and sailboat both get their motion through
operating in the air. The sailboat uses the energy of the
wind. The hovercraft uses an air propeller to push itself
forward. In a way, the concept of the sailing ship is different
from all the others, because it requires no added input of
energy, but relies on the natural energy of the wind.

▶ *if he or she can see a
"concept connection"
between the cards. The
players can agree to
exclude some simple
connections, such
as "both contain
some metal."*

*The same concept
connection should not
be made more than
once in each game.
The player who says
"snap" first and then
follows it up with
an explanation of
the concept
connection takes all
the cards from the
other player that have
been turned over
up to that point. The
game continues until
one player has no
cards left or until
an agreed time
has been reached.
The player with
the most cards
wins the game.*

One player picks a
card at random from
the pack and places it
face up on the table.
Each player in turn
has to suggest a
concept that includes
the item on the card.

The concept must be
related in some way
to the function of the
item. Each new
concept can be
broader or narrower
than the previous one.
But if the new concept
makes too big a jump,
then the next player
can suggest a concept
that is in between
the new concept and
the previous one. ▶

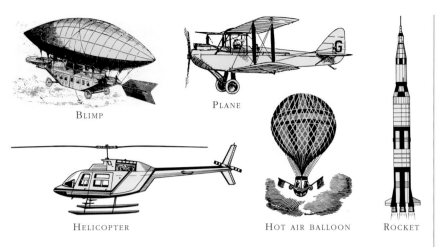

BLIMP

PLANE

HELICOPTER

HOT AIR BALLOON

ROCKET

ALL THESE THINGS CAN move through the air. Some of the
similarities are easy to recognize. For example, the blimp and the hot
air balloon are both lighter than air, and the plane and the helicopter
both fly using wings. But what are the different concepts involved?
And why is the rocket different from the other four?

Check for suggestions on pages 70-71 ☞

A son has a father but the father

is the son of someone else.

And that father is *also* a son.

In the same way, a CONCEPT

may define a GROUP but may

also be part of a second and

LARGER GROUP – and so on.

▶ *For example, if the
item on the card is a
bucket, player A
might suggest: "a
way of transporting
water." Player B
might suggest a
narrower concept: "a
portable container for
water." A concept in
between the two might
be: "getting water to
where you need it."
Once every player has
suggested a concept,
the game continues
with a new card.*

COMMENT

A variant of this game
is as follows: turn over
a card, agree on a
concept; turn over
another card and find a
concept that links the
two. You will improve
each time you play.

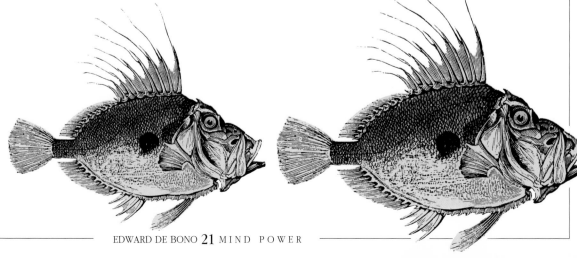

WHAT COULD IT BE?

possibilities

We like to be certain. We like to be sure. We want to know that what we are eating is definitely an edible mushroom and not, in fact, a poisonous toadstool.

Yet possibilities are the

DRIVING FORCE of human thinking

and human *progress*.

A   B   C

WHAT ARE THE OBJECTS shown in this distorted way?

Check your answers on pages 70-71 ☞

Possibilities allow us to deal with new or old things that we cannot see clearly. We may come up with a possibility in our minds and then work to check that possibility out.

A

B

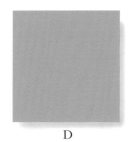

C

D

E

AMONG THE FIVE SHAPES SHOWN above, one does not belong. Which one could it be and why? Check your answers on pages 70-71 ☞

Possibilities and guessing go hand in hand. We naturally prefer to work from certainty rather than from a guess. But the guess gives us something to work on, so that we can eventually arrive at certainty.

In the above exercise, we need to work out which shape doesn't belong. We start by making a guess. Then we check this guess against the other shapes. If it turns out that none of the other shapes possess the "guessed" feature, then we can say that this is at least one of the reasons that the shape has been chosen.

Science works in exactly the same way. There is evidence, data, or information. Then someone makes a guess as to what is going on. In science, this type of possibility is called a hypothesis. We can then look at the evidence through this hypothesis to see if things fit. We can look for more evidence to check out the hypothesis. We can design experiments to check out the hypothesis.

Sometimes, we cannot move from possibility to certainty. The best we can do is move from possibilty to probability.

THINKARD GAME
THE DISCOVERY GAME

The cards are laid face up on the table. One player chooses a card because the object shown on the card contains a particular feature (for example: "It has wheels"; "It needs electricity.") The other player has to carry out "experiments" in order to find the hidden feature. This player is the "experimenter."

The experimenter chooses a card that he or she thinks may contain the hidden feature. This is put forward as an "experiment." The ▶

▶ *first player says "yes" or "no," depending on whether the experiment card contains the hidden feature. The successful cards are placed on the same level as the original card.*

The unsuccessful cards are placed a level below. When the experimenter thinks that he or she has the answer, this is put forward.

This game can be made very difficult if the first player chooses two features instead of just one. For example: "It needs electricity to work and can be useful in the garden." This more difficult version of the game should only be used after much experience with the simpler version in which there is only one hidden feature.

In technology, there is a "vision" of a possibility. Then we set out to find ways of making that possibility happen. The tunnel under the Channel separating England from France was somebody's vision. Then ways of making it happen had to be worked out in detail.

THE PICTURE SHOWS a box standing on its edge on a table. There is no support. Why is the box standing on its corner? Can you make a box do the same thing? You are not allowed to attach the box to the table in any way. Check your answers on pages 70-71 ☞

In the above exercise, there are two things that you may want to know. The first thing is how this particular box has been made to stand on its edge. The second thing is how any box can be made to stand on its edge. In the second case, you may be able to design other ways of doing it that are totally different from the one that has actually been used. The first case is like science. You set out to discover what is actually happening. The second case is more like technology. You create new possibilities.

NUMBER
CARD GAME
**THE
SEQUENCE
GAME**

*One player chooses
a sequence of four
numbers: for example,
3 - 7 - 11 - 15. The
other person has to
produce as many
possibilities as he or
she can for the choice
of this sequence. The
relationship between
the numbers must, of
course, be consistent
and should not
change as the
sequence develops.*

*Note that the sequence
is all-important.
It is not a matter
of putting together
numbers that just
happen to have some
feature in common.
In the example given,
you simply add four
to one number to
get the next number.
In the sequence
4 - 7 - 13 - 25, you
add the number* ▶

The brain can only see what it has been *prepared* to see. So unless we prepare the brain by *creating possibilities,* we are unable to see NEW PATTERNS and NEW IDEAS.

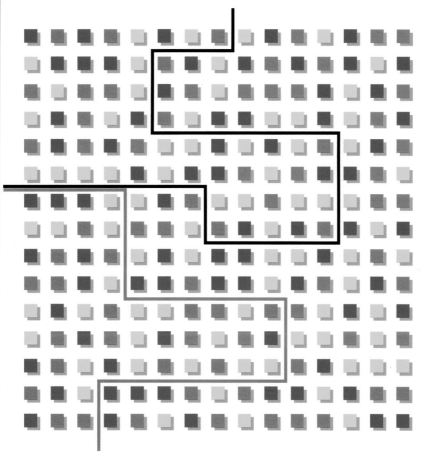

THE DIAGRAM ABOVE shows a maze. Imagine that a robot cart has been programmed to find its ways through the maze by following certain rules. The black line shows one route that the cart has taken. The red line shows the route that is taken when the rules have been changed. What are the two sets of rules? Check your answers on pages 70-71 ☞

It is only when we have discovered or created a range of possibilities that we are adequately prepared to exercise our judgment.

▶ *to itself and then
subtract one. The basis
of the sequence may
be quite complex.*

*The Sequence Game
works differently for
each player. The
player who is trying to
find the sequence is in
the position of a
scientist who is trying
to discover the "truth"
or "possible truths."*

*When playing the
Number Card games
for the first time, use
cards 1–20. When
playing the games on
subsequent occasions,
use as many of the
cards as you wish.*

COMMENT

Once you have
worked out the two
different sets of rules,
devise your own set
of rules for crossing
the maze.

judgment

In some ways, judgment is the most fundamental operation of human thinking.

does this match?
DOES THIS FIT?
is this right?

In our minds we have an idea of how things should be. We then judge whether something matches this idea. Recognition is based on judgment. You see an unusual-looking cat or dog. Does this match your mental picture of a cat or dog? Or does it challenge it? If you are the expert judge at a dog show, you choose the winning animal by seeing which dog best matches the "right" shape for each different breed.

Experience gives us mental pictures of how things work and what happens under different circumstances. We then judge whether our actions are "right" depending upon whether these actions fit our mental pictures.

DOES THIS Sphynx cat match your mental picture of a cat?

DOES THIS Neapolitan mastiff match your mental picture of a dog?

There are rules in playing any game. There are traffic rules. There are rules of law. There are rules of grammar and rules of mathematics. We judge whether something is "right" depending on whether it follows or matches those rules.

THE LINES SHOWN BELOW are of different widths and different colours. Their positions are different. Can you "judge" which of these lines are equal in length to line A? Do not use any measuring method. Do it by eye. Check your answers on pages 70-71 ☞

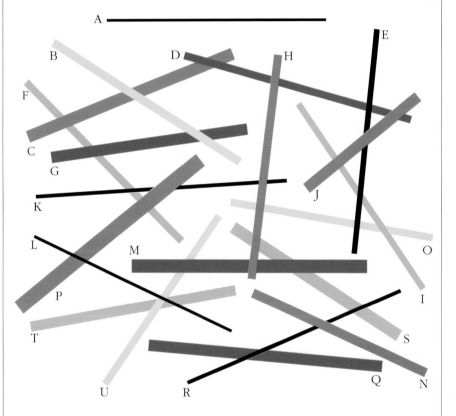

Though we often pretend otherwise, judgment of many things is not always easy. There are "maybe" situations. We may have to make a DECISION. Sometimes the decision is not as firmly based as we would like.

T H I N K A R D
G A M E
**JUDGED
PAIRS**

———

The pack of cards is shuffled and then cut. Twenty cards are laid face up on the table. The task is to pick out three pairs. Each pair must be based on usefulness.

———

You might judge, for example, that "This card would help the other one to carry out its function." The pairing should not be made on the basis of features, concepts, or similarity, but only on the basis of synergy.

———

Each player makes a mental note of his or her pairs and then these are revealed together. They can also be written down and then revealed.

THINKARD
GAME
**MEMORY
JUDGMENT**

Sixteen cards are laid
face up in
a four-by-four grid.
The players observe
the cards for 20
seconds. The cards
are then turned
face down.

Each player takes
turns predicting the
card he or she is about
to turn over. If the
prediction is correct,
the player keeps the
card. If the prediction
is wrong, the opponent
gets the card. ▶

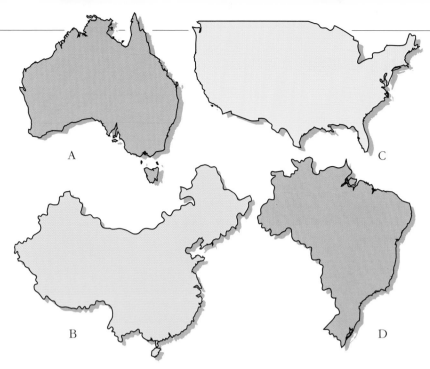

A

B

C

D

CAN YOU IDENTIFY the countries above by their shapes and sizes? The possibilities are: Brazil, Australia, Canada, Argentina, Russia, China, and the United States. Check your answers on pages 70-71 ☞

Every time we judge something, we are judging it against some EXPERIENCE or EXPECTATION or *feeling*. A scientist has a *feeling* for his or her subject. A cook has a *feeling* of what tastes right.

▶ The game continues
until no cards are left.
The winner is the
player with most cards.

This game can also be
played in another way.
Two players each lay
out a set of 12 cards
face up. After 20
seconds, the cards
are turned face
down. A player now
seeks to identify the
card of the opponent.
If the guess is correct,
then that player gets
the card. If the
identification is
wrong, the card stays
face down. The
owner of the card can
look at it to check if
the guess is right.

The game continues
until either player has
five more cards
than the opponent.

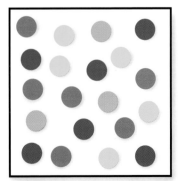
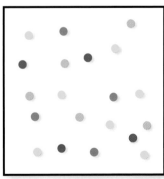
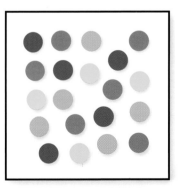
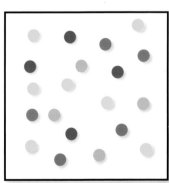

HERE ARE FOUR squares, each containing a number of dots. Which do you judge to have the most dots? Put the squares in descending order, from the most dots to the least. Check your answers on pages 70-71 ☞

FRAME OF
JUDGMENT

*One player writes
down a possible frame
of judgment. Some
examples are: "would
make a good birthday
present"; "useful in the
kitchen"; "dangerous if
you are not careful";
"requires skill to use."*

*This piece of paper is
then placed face
down on the table.
The opponent now
turns over the cards
one by one. The first
player has to judge
instantly whether ▶*

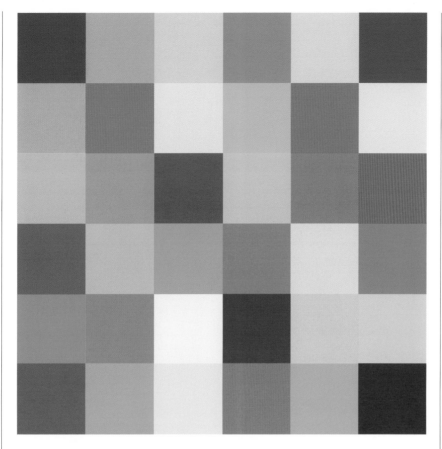

THE ABOVE PICTURE shows a selection of different colors.
Which of the colors above exactly match the six used below?

Check your answers on pages 70-71 ☞

▶ *the turned-up card
fits the frame of
judgment. So two piles
grow: the
accepted items and
the rejected items.
The person making
the judgments wins
if the number of cards
in the acceptance pile
is greater than 15.
Otherwise, the
opponent wins.*

*After the game is over,
the opponent can
challenge a particular
judgment by reading
the judgment frame
from the piece of
paper and pointing
out that one or
more cards do not
match this frame.
This is to prevent a
player from cheating
in order to reach
the required
number of cards.*

The most important aspect of judgment is to *know what you are seeking to match.* It is one thing to match something against a formal definition or rule, but it is another thing to match something against the needs of the moment. Those needs can form a complex frame of judgment. For instance, a diner might judge a restaurant menu with the following frame in mind: "I want something that is meat, not fish, and that does not have a heavy sauce with it." A choice is made according to whether an item on the menu matches that frame of judgment. If not, a compromise has to be made.

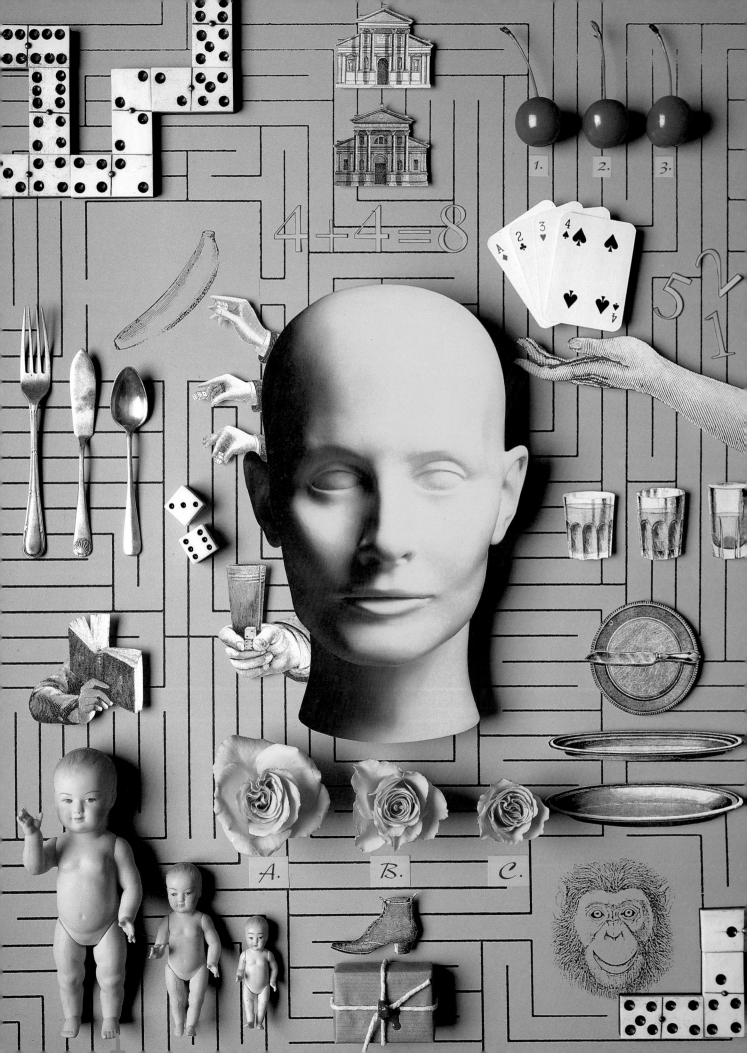

4+4=8

1. 2. 3.

5 2
1

A.   B.   C.

alternatives
alternatives

You may wish to have dinner at an Italian restaurant or, alternatively, at a Japanese restaurant. You get to the restaurant and look at the menu. The menu lists alternative dishes that you can choose.

A baby is expected. Sometimes the parents know exactly the name that thay are going to give to their new son or daughter. It may be a traditional family name.

At other times, the parents discuss several alternative names. They may purchase a book that lists hundreds of alternative names. They can then gradually eliminate alternatives, until, finally, they have a list of just four or fewer names from which to choose.

*Shuffle the pack of
cards. Take the top
four cards and lay
them face up
on the table in the
sequence in which
they were turned up.*

*Now construct a story
around that sequence
so that each item on
the cards comes into
the story in the right
order. Next try to
construct another
story for the same
sequence of cards.
Now change the
sequence around,
as you wish, and
construct a third story.
Change the sequence
again and find a
new story.*

*You can play this
game on your own
or with someone else.
It is up to you to be
satisfied with your
own story.*

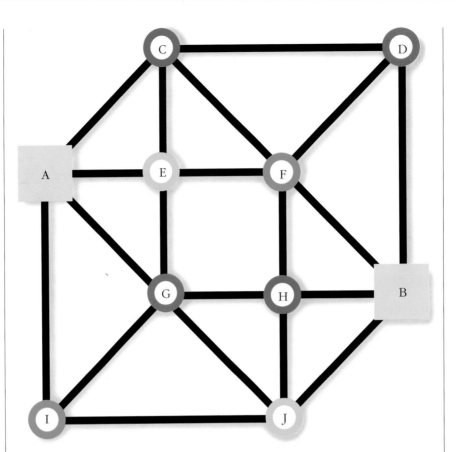

THE PICTURE SHOWS a type of maze. You start at point A and finish at point B. What are the alternative routes if you must visit exactly four other points on the way? You cannot visit the same point more than once. Check your answers on pages 70-71 ☞

To make the
Alternative Stories
game more difficult,
you could deal out
more cards. Or add a
card into the middle of
a story and adapt the
story accordingly.

At a traffic circle, the sign lists several ALTERNATIVE ROADS that you can take. You quickly try to figure out *which alternative would serve your purpose.*

Alternatives must serve the same purpose. A rose is not an alternative to a pair of shoes. We might, however, imagine a circumstance in which both a rose and a pair of shoes are being considered as alternative gifts. In this case, they would both serve the purpose of "giving a present."

Sometimes alternatives are presented to you, but at other times you have to create alternatives for yourself. If the alternatives are presented, then all you have to do is choose between them. This would be the case when you are choosing from a menu in a restaurant. In other cases, you have to create possible alternatives first and then choose from them. This would be the case if you were cooking for yourself.

FOUR TILES containing numbers and either an addition or subtraction sign are shown below. Write down five different ways in which you could reach the total of 22. You can try this using each number as often as you like. For instance, you could use +4 six times and then use -2 once.

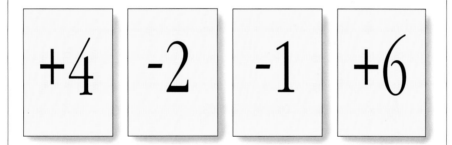

In many of the situations presented in this chapter, it is easy to check whether the alternative is a valid alternative. In the above exercise, for instance, you can test directly whether the proposed alternative fits the conditions that have been given. Four plus four equals eight. Five plus two plus one equals eight. But six plus three does not equal eight.

In other cases, however, the answer is not so easy. It may be a matter of individual judgment as to whether what is proposed is really an alternative. If you are thirsty and I offer you water or orange juice, those might be alternatives. But if I offer beer, that might be an alternative for some people, but not an alternative for others who do not drink beer.

THINKARD
GAME
**LOGICAL
SEQUENCE**

Shuffle the pack and then deal out five cards face up. Arrange these five cards in some sort of logical sequence. This should not be a story.

There must be some logical connection between one card and the next one. It is enough that there is a logical connection between the first card and the second card and that there is a different logical connection between the second card and the third card. In how many alternative ways can you arrange the sequence?

NUMBER
CARD GAME
**NUMBER
SEQUENCE
ALTERNATIVES**

*Shuffle the pack
and place it face
down. Turn over the
cards one by one until
two numbers in a
sequence are turned
up, one after the
other. Place these
cards side by side
to form the base
of the sequence.*

*Continue to turn over
the cards. A new card
may increase the
sequence upward or
downward. For
example, if the
established sequence
is 7 - 8, then either
6 or 9 can be added
to the sequence.
Cards that do not fit ▶*

In some situations, there are two levels of alternatives. The first level involves a search through our minds to find a possible logical connection between two situations or items. This means creating and considering alternatives. The second level is the search for different logical connections.

Usually, we look for alternatives only until we have found one that satisfies our needs of the moment. This is not good thinking. We need to look for other possible alternatives even when we already have one that works. There is no reason at all to believe that the first satisfactory alternative that we find is the best possible one.

We should always try to find BETTER ALTERNATIVES, even when we are already considering something that works very well. *Finding better alternatives is how improvement and progress come about.*

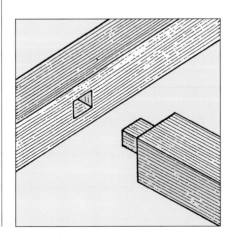

THE PICTURE shows one method of attaching two pieces of wood to each other: joinery. Which alternative methods can you think of that would accomplish the same task? Check for possible answers on pages 70-71 ☞

*▶ the sequence are
discarded face up
on the table.*

*At any moment the
player can switch
from the first
established sequence to
a new sequence made
from the discarded
cards on the table. But
the cards used in the
first sequence cannot
be reused. Following
these conditions,
another sequence
may be started. The
cards in the old
sequence remain
unusable.*

*The game ends when
all the cards in the
pack have been
turned over. The
objective is to build
old (or new)
sequences for as long
as possible without
having to discard a
card. To do this, the
player has to keep
an eye on emerging
sequences and then
switch to one of them.*

It is not an easy task to find all the possible alternatives that there are in a given situation. In some cases there may be so many alternatives to discover that the task would be impossible.

It is always worthwhile, however, to go beyond the obvious alternatives that are presented. This extra effort might well produce an original and valuable alternative that has not been included. This extra work might reveal an alternative to you that is just as acceptable and valid in the situation.

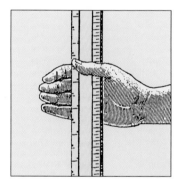 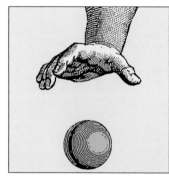 

THE PICTURES SHOW three different ways of finding out the height of a building: measuring one story and multiplying that measurement as appropriate; dropping an object from the top of the building and timing its fall; lowering a string from the top of the building. What other ways can you think of? Which is the most efficient method? Which method would you choose? Pause and do your own thinking before reading further.

In the exercise featured above, the obvious alternatives are those that involve physically measuring the building with an appropriate measuring device, or alternatively, calculating the dimensions of the building by a mathematical method. You may consider measuring the shadow and working out the height of the building from that information if the circumstances allow. Or you could ask the architect.

a.   b.   c.

comparison & choice

There are, of course, two aspects of comparison.

WHAT IS *different?*
WHAT IS THE SAME?

For many years scientists believed that an all-green and an all-red variety of an Australasian parrot were actually different species. Eventually they discovered that the green and red birds were male and female of the Eclectus species.

COMPARISON

enables us

to *move*

forward to

new things.

We come across something that is new. We look to see what there is about it that is "the same" as something we already know. This allows us to treat the new thing, cautiously, as we would have treated the thing we know. Then we start to focus on the differences between the new thing and the thing we know. Finally, we create a new "box" for the new thing, and thereafter we can read it in terms of its own box (see page 17.)

Science is based on using both these questions. For example, in the first analysis, a whale appears to be totally different from a human being. Yet if we analyze the two in more depth, there are strong points of similarity. They both breathe air, they are both warm-blooded, they both give birth to live young – in fact, they are both mammals. Whales may also have an elaborate system of communication. Though sharks and dolphins look similar, dolphins are part of the whale family. Things that seem the same can be very different. Things that look different can be the same. New species are discovered this way. This is called "lumping" and "splitting." You lump together things that seem different, and split apart things that seem the same.

FLOWERS that may seem very different can turn out to have so much in common that they belong to the same species. To which species do these two flowers belong? For the answer see pages 70–71 ☞

SPERM WHALE

BABY

GREAT WHITE SHARK

Dinosaurs seem very different from birds, but there is good evidence to suggest that birds descended from dinosaurs. When there are existing

ROBIN

COMPSOGNATHUS

alternatives, or whenever we generate possible alternatives, we often compare them to see which one might be better. There may be two routes up a mountain. One is faster and more direct, but more dangerous. The other is slower, but easier and safer to climb. Which one you decide to choose will depend on your needs or personality.

Sometimes it is necessary to look hard in order to find small points of difference. In such cases, you set your mind to look for differences, and then you will find them. It does not mean that these differences are significant. People have different-shaped ears. This point of difference has no practical value. An often-used method for dismissing a new idea is to claim that the new idea is "the same as" the existing idea. In such cases, there is a need to focus on the difference between the new idea and the old one; it may seem small, but can lead in a whole new direction.

THINKARD
GAME
**THE
SIMILARITY
GAME**

Shuffle the pack. Deal out two sets of five cards face down, placing the cards in parallel columns. The cards are now turned over. The task is to

pick out a pair of cards, one from each column, which have many things in common. You have two choices for similarity: either choose aspects that are strongly held in common; or you can list aspects that are held in common, but not in a dominant way. You can choose different pairs for each approach.

THINKARD
GAME
**THE
DIFFERENCE
GAME**

Shuffle the pack. Turn over the cards two at a time. For each pair the player lists the points of difference. This may seem like an easy game because the items on the cards are clearly different. It is necessary to get beyond the simple points of difference such as shape, size, and color.

It becomes more difficult as you try to point out contrasts in function. For example: "This makes things bigger. . . This makes things smaller." Such functional contrasts are more valuable than just saying, "This can be used in the yard, and this can be used in the kitchen."

NUMBER CARD GAME

THE ADJACENT GAME

Deal out the cards, face up, in a line. Stop when any two adjacent cards add up to a total given by any other two adjacent cards. If there are two players or more, then the first player to spot the "similarity" is the winner. Take turns dealing.

KITTEN   BIRD   FISH

TURTLE   DOG   RABBIT

IMAGINE YOU ARE considering keeping one of these animals as a pet. Compare them to one another as pairs. Focus on the points of difference.

CHOICE and DECISION are tied up with *alternatives, comparison,* and *judgment.* Without choice there are no alternatives. We judge which alternative is best.

COMPARE THREE DIFFERENT ways of getting to work: car, bus, and motorcycle. Consider points such as the following: you can read on a bus; you don't have to wait for a car or a motorcycle; a bus may be cheaper. Make a list of five negative points and five positive points about each mode of transport.

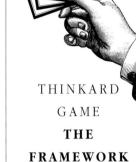

THINKARD GAME

THE FRAMEWORK GAME

Shuffle the pack and then turn over the top card in the pack. Look at this card and ask yourself the following question: "Under what conditions and in what frame of mind would I choose the item shown on this card?"

Repeat this process until you have chosen two more cards that might fit the same framework. Now that you have three possible alternatives, make a choice between the three.

MOTORCYCLE

CAR

BUS

This is a game for two players. The pack is shuffled and three cards are dealt to each of the players, who look at their cards but hide them from their opponent.

Each player in turn exposes the top card of the face-down pack. The player has to decide whether to keep that card or to discard it. Each player may hold only five cards at any time. So when a player has five cards, he or she can only take a new card if an old ▶

Decision is a form of choice. The minimum choice is between doing something and not doing something: to buy a camera or not to buy a camera. There may be a third option: to postpone buying a camera. There may be a fourth option: to think further about buying a camera. The decision not to do something is still a decision, even though it often arises from the inability to make a decision.

There are always two aspects to any decision or choice.

the first aspect

is an exploration of the alternatives available. This may be an attempt to discover more alternatives. It may be possible to design a new alternative that combines two of the other alternatives. What would be the consequences of choosing a particular alternative? We would look at the immediate and longer-term consequences. We would look at the difficulties, problems, and potential dangers.

the second aspect

has to do entirely with the person who is making the particular choice or decision. What are the needs of that person? What are his or her tastes? What is the context of the choice? What are the priorities involved? What are the values? What is the objective or goal that must be reached in making the choice or decision?

▶ one is discarded. A player may turn over a fresh card from the pack and take this card, or may instead pick up the discarded card of the other player. The winner is the first player to obtain a sequence of four cards. If this proves too difficult, then a sequence of three cards is acceptable.

In this game, each player has to make an immediate decision: "Do I require this card or not?" This will depend on the cards the player already holds in his or her hand, and also on what he or she thinks the other player is collecting. There may also be another decision to be made: "Which card do I discard?"

analysis

Analysis is one of the most fundamental processes of human thinking. How can you break down a complicated situation into smaller sections that you recognize? In every field, analysis is a key activity. Many things in the world are quite complicated. Most things that we know are quite simple. So we have to break down the complicated matters into the simple things that we know and can deal with more easily.

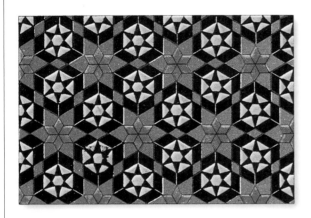

LOOK CLOSELY at this Islamic design, and you will see how a complex pattern can be created from surprisingly few simple shapes.

Success in thinking often depends on success in analysis. But there are two big dangers. Too many people are taught to believe that analysis and judgment are enough. They are not. Creativity and possibilities are the driving forces of progress. The other danger is that the behavior of a complex system cannot be detected in the behavior of its parts. If you chop an animal into pieces, you no longer have a functioning animal.

THIS SQUARE has been made from the pieces shown beside it, without any overlapping. No piece has been used more than once. Not all the pieces have been used. Which pieces have been used to construct the shape? For the answer see pages 70-71 ☞

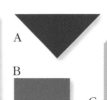

A
B
C
D
E
F

*One player looks
through the cards in
the pack and puts
together a collection
of four cards. There
must be some reason
for this collection.
The reason cannot
be a story told
around the cards.*

*The reason should be
written down on a
piece of paper. The
second player has to
analyze the reason
behind the* ▶

Despite the dangers, analysis is a VERY IMPORTANT PART of thinking.

LOOK CAREFULLY at these laid-out pieces of wood and decide which item of furniture could be assembled from them.
Check your answers on pages 70-71 ☞

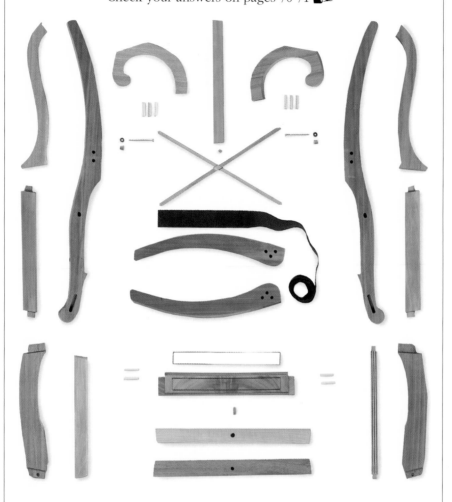

▶ *collection. This can
be done in two ways:
1. The player can
choose another card
and offer it. The
response could be: "It
fits"; "It might just fit";
"It definitely does
not fit."
2. The player can ask
a question that can be
answered by a simple
"yes" or "no."*

*Offering a card
counts as one point.
Asking a direct
question counts as
three points. Only
15 points can be
accumulated. Guesses
count as a question,
except that a final
guess can be made
after the 15 points
have been used up.
The two players then
reverse their roles.*

Sometimes the parts are separate and have been brought together to form a whole. For example, a carpenter cuts the pieces of wood that he or she wants and then assembles them into a piece of furniture.

At other times, the parts are not separate but overlapping. It is still a matter of sorting out the different elements that have gone into the final situation.

NUMBER
CARD GAME
**ANALYZING
ACHIEVEMENT**

_____

*The pack is shuffled
and five cards are
dealt out face up. Is
there any way in
which four of the
cards can be arranged
so as to provide the
value of the
remaining card?*

_____

*You can use
addition, subtraction,
multiplication, or
division, but you must
deal in whole
numbers only. You
can use only the given
cards. Whichever
player first spots a
way of achieving the
objective wins.*

_____

*If no one can see a
way, then a new card
is turned over and
one of the existing
five cards is discarded.
The game continues
until one player finds
a way of achieving
the task.*

In analyzing complex situations, with many connected parts, there is often a need to think of things that are not physically present, but those that exist in our minds.

THIS PICTURE SHOWS traffic congestion in a city. Analyze the factors involved: the causes, potential solutions, the rights and wrongs of the situation. Pause and do your own thinking before reading further.

The factors you might have analyzed include: the size of the roads; the need for travel and traffic; car ownership; the design and layout of the city; parking facilities; the enforcement of traffic regulations; the need to deliver goods in the city; and the behavior of pedestrians.

IMAGINE SOMEONE preparing a meal in a kitchen. Analyze the stages involved in preparing a meal. Pause and do your own thinking before reading further.

Your analysis might have included some of the following points – and some additional ones: deciding on the number of courses; deciding what each course will be; choosing which ingredients to use; deciding how much money to spend; getting the ingredients; preparing the ingredients; grouping the things that need to be cooked together; deciding what sequence to cook them in; putting things together; arranging presentation so that the food looks good; keeping it warm; deciding what time to eat; deciding where to eat; making the seating arrangements; and finally, serving the meal.

There are times when an analysis *reveals the true parts* that are present or that have been assembled into the FINAL SITUATION. But there are other occasions when the parts are determined by *how we choose to look* at something. This is what we call PERCEPTION.

perception

Perception is by far *the most important part* of thinking. Perception is *the way we see the world* around us at any particular moment.

All perception is based on experience. Perception is based on our mood, our needs of the moment, and on our thinking skills.

When we see a plate of chicken and vegetables, our experience tells us what it is. Our experience reminds us how chicken and vegetables taste. But the way we see it also depends on ourselves. If we are hungry, we see it as attractive. If we have just eaten, then the chicken is much less attractive. If we know that there is a salmonella scare and that most chicken is infected, then we view the plate with suspicion. Our thinking skills direct our attention, and so affect our perception. We can direct our attention to the benefits and drawbacks of eating that chicken. As a result, we may make a decision.

THINKARD
GAME
**THE
PERCEPTION
GAME**

———

*This game is played by
two or more people.
Shuffle the pack. Turn
over one card and
place it face up on
the table. Ten more
cards are dealt and
turned face up.*

———

*From these cards, each
player then chooses a
card that fits in with a
principle that he or
she has chosen based
on the first card. So
one player forms a
group to the right of
the original card.* ▶

THE PICTURE SHOWS an outline shape. How would you describe this shape? Try to think of as many alternatives as you can. Pause and do your own thinking before reading further.

You could see the picture as being made up of two overlapping squares. You could stop with that, or your thinking skills could urge you to look for more possibilities, more alternatives. Thinking further, you could see the picture as a three-dimensional drawing of two squares, one standing in front of the other. You could also see the shape as two L-shaped pieces. You may find even more ways.

Which way of looking at something is the "RIGHT" one?

In some cases, there is a "right" answer when we are trying to recognize something. When you are driving and notice something strange on the road ahead, it is very important that your perception is "right." In many cases, however, perception is a matter of choice. Perception opens up possibilities. We can choose one of these, or we can explore several possibilities.

THE PICTURE SHOWS a triangle of coins. The triangle is pointing up. How can you get the triangle to point down? Move the smallest number of coins you can in order to achieve this. Check your answers on pages 70-71 ☞

▶ *The other player
forms a group to the
left. Each player must
have a basis for the
grouping, for example,
"things that are used
in the garden." The
basis cannot be a
story.*

———

*Each player in turn
picks a card from the
cards lying face up
and adds it to their
group. Cards not
selected are put aside.
A new set of ten cards
is dealt face up.
The game ends when
there are no cards left
in the pack.*

———

*Without questioning,
each player has five
chances to guess the
basis for the group of
the other player. The
answer may be "yes,"
"no," or, if the guess is
almost right, "close."*

THINKARD
GAME
**CHANGE
PERCEPTION
GAME**

_The pack is shuffled
and one card is drawn
and placed face up
on the table.
One player describes
in very simple terms
the nature or function
of the item on the
card. The other player
has to describe the
item in a different
way. For example,_ ▶

THIS PICTURE SHOWS some empty circles and some filled-in circles. How many filled-in circles does the picture show? Pause and think before reading further.

How did you reach your conclusion? Check your answers on pages 70-71 ☞

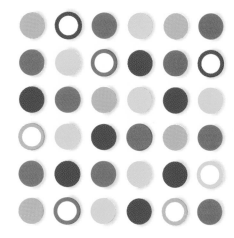

▶ _if the item was
a hose, one
player might say:
"A way of directing
water to a specific
place." The other
player might say:
"A way to avoid
wasting water where
it is not wanted."_

_This can be a difficult
game, and it does not
work equally well for
all items. Sometimes
the "changed"
perception is not
a true change but
a different aspect.
The important point
is to try. If one card
does not work well,
then move on to
the next card._

Perception is concerned with change. How can we see the same thing in many different ways? You can look at a glass of fruit juice and say that it is half full. You can look at the same glass and say that it is half empty.

You see two people running, one after the other. In how many different ways could you look at this scene? Before reading further, write out a list of five possible interpretations. Then compare these with the interpretations that follow, and try to add some more.

1. One person is trying to catch the other.

2. One person is trying to escape from the other.

3. They are both running away from something.

4. They are both running toward something or someone.

5. It has just started to rain and they are both running for shelter.

WHAT DOES THE PICTURE above depict? A fierce dog? Two cars heading toward each other that are about to collide? How else could the dog and the cars be perceived?

COMMENT

You may think that the dog looks threatening, but it would be less so if you knew it was behind a fence.

NUMBER CARD GAME
NUMBER CHOICE

The pack of cards is shuffled and a card is dealt to each of the players in turn. If the value of the card is 12 or higher, then that card is placed face up in front of the player and no more cards are dealt to that player. This part of the game continues ▶

THE PICTURE ABOVE SHOWS a grid of painted squares. How many squares do you see?
Check your answers on pages 70-71 ☞

COMMENT

The two cars look as if they might collide, but equally they could be stationary or reversing.

▶ *until each player has a card valued at 12 or higher in front of him or her. All the remaining cards are collected and reshuffled.*

Each player now decides how the card in front of him or her can be broken down into a sum of three (only three) other numbers. For example, 12 can be broken down into 6 + 4 + 2. For this game, there is no advantage to having two numbers be the same.

Cards are now turned over one by one ▶

In many sitiuations, the change in our perception depends on what our minds choose to bring to the situation as possibilities. We might wish to broaden our perception. This is an important aspect of perception. How widely do we look? What other things do we take into account?

▶ *from the pack. Each player in turn is asked if he or she can "accept" that card. A player can only accept a card if one of three cases occurs:*

1. The card is exactly equal to one of any of the player's broken-up numbers (for example, 6 or 4 or 2 in the case of 12.)

2. The card is equal to a combination of any of the broken-up numbers (for example, 6 + 2 = 8 in the case of 12.)

3. The card is equal to any combination of ▶

THIS DETAIL FROM A PAINTING contains items of many different colors. Close your eyes and tell yourself you are going to look at red items. Now look at the picture. Repeat the exercise with yellow items, white items, and then with blue items. Each time you do this you will see the painting in a totally new way.

One very important aspect of perception is SELECTION. *What are the things that we choose to look at?* Where do we DIRECT our attention?

Sometimes there are things that immediately catch our attention. At other times our attention flows from one thing to another. There are times when we need some framework for directing attention deliberately. This is what the CoRT Program (see page 72) for the direct teaching of thinking in schools is all about.

▶ *the broken-up numbers added to the original number (for example, 12 + 2 or 12 + 6 + 4 in the case of 12.)*

A player does not have to declare the broken-up numbers that he or she decides upon; however, the player may be challenged about his or her choices at the end of the game.

The game ends when there are no more cards left in the pack. The player with the most cards wins the game.

values & feelings

In the end, values and feelings are the *most important* things *to anyone* who is doing any THINKING.

Values and feelings determine our objectives. Is this worth achieving? Why is this worth achieving? Values and feelings strongly affect our judgment of people, of things, and of courses of action. Values and feelings determine whether we are satisfied with the outcome of our thinking.

Does this mean that we should not bother to think but just depend on our feelings? Not at all.

The purpose of thinking is to arrange the world in our minds, so that we can APPLY our feelings EFFECTIVELY – not only for ourselves but *for other people, too.*

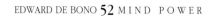

THINKARD
GAME
QUICK VALUES

The object of this game is to choose five cards that have the highest value for you. The game is best played with two players. One player turns over the cards rapidly from the face-down pack.

Each card of the pack is shown to the second player, who is allowed about three seconds to view each card and to decide whether to select it as one of his or her "valuable" five.

The player is not allowed to change his or her mind or go back to choose a card that has passed. All values are allowed except financial values. At the end of the game, the player must explain the value of each choice to the other player.

Feelings may tell you to fight someone with whom you disagree. Thinking may design an outcome that is satisfactory to both sides. There is nothing more dangerous than to assume that values and feelings without thinking are enough. Many of the world's wars and persecutions have arisen in this way.

Without thought, feelings and values are dangerous. There are three important things that we need to consider:

the first thing

is to acknowledge and to be aware of what our values and feelings are in a situation.

the second thing

is to see how those values and feelings affect our thinking with regard to the situation.

the third thing

is to consider whether the values and feelings are justified or helpful in a particular situation.

THINKARD
GAME
CONSTRUCTIVE VALUES

In this game, the values have to fit together to achieve some purpose. Six cards are dealt to a player. These cards are exposed face up.

The player has to show how four of these cards can be used together to set up a business. This can be a business that makes money, or it can be an operation that provides value to the community.

Players work cooperatively in this game, each offering suggestions. Once again, the value of selling one of the items on the cards to raise money or to make money is not permitted, because it would make the game much too easy.

NUMBER CARD GAME
EARLY CHOICE

This is a two-person game. The pack is shuffled and placed face down. Each player is then dealt one card, which is exposed. Each player in turn exposes a card from the pack. The player may keep this card or reject it. For each player, the first two cards accepted are placed alongside the first card to form a group of three cards. The sum total of the three cards is noted.

The objective of each player is to form as many groups as possible with a value that is the same as this first group or close to it. Players must now use the card that they expose. There are no more discards. A card may either be added to an existing group or may form ▶

There are at least two big problems with values and feelings. The first problem is that your values and feelings may not agree with the values and feelings of other people. They may not agree with those of society in general or those of a particular group. For example, environmentalists may have very different values and feelings from industrialists.

LOOK AT THE SIX different chairs pictured below. What do you feel about each of them? Note your feelings before reading further.

Now put yourself in the position of someone opening a new restaurant. Look at each chair again and note your feelings under these new circumstances. What are the values now involved? You might consider cost, convenience, ease of cleaning, sturdiness, and contribution to atmosphere.

The second problem with values and feelings is that something that has a high value at the moment might have a negative value later. The next drink at a party seems very attractive. But if you have an auto accident later or are stopped for drunk driving, then there are a lot of negative values.

▶ *the start of a new group. Once placed in a position on the table, a card may not then be shifted to a new group. When the pack is exhausted, all the cards that are not in a completed group are collected and shuffled again to form a new pack. The game continues until the new pack is also exhausted.*

The scoring is as follows:
• *Completed groups score 20 points.*
• *If a new group does not match the total of the first group, then the difference is subtracted from 20 to give a score for that group.*
• *Single cards are always counted as a minus score according to their face value. This score is subtracted from the total score.*

The player with the highest score at the end is the winner. The point of the game is that the player has to choose right at the beginning the most useful "value" for the first group.

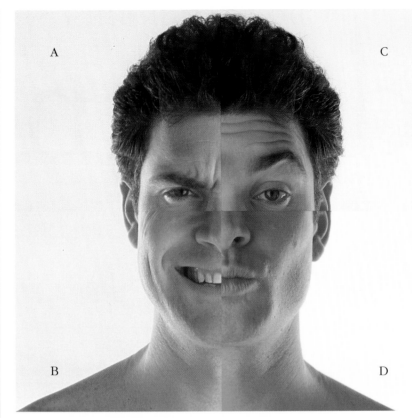

A   C

B   D

LOOK AT THE FOUR quarters of this face. What is your
first impression? Now try to recognize the different
feelings that are being expressed.
Check your answers on pages 70-71 ☞

It can also work the other way around. It might be a bore
and a nuisance for a child to brush his or her teeth, but later
there can be benefits. It is hard to study for exams when all
your friends are out having a good time. But later, when you
have graduated, you may end up doing better than them.

Being sensitive to the feelings of others is part of the
importance of feelings. To do that, we need to recognize the
feelings of others. Some people are better at it than others.

There are, of course, negative values and positive values.
These may differ from person to person and may also
depend on the circumstances.

THINKARD
GAME
**DIFFERENT
VALUES**

———

*The pack is shuffled
and the top card is
given to one player.
The card is placed face
up on the table.*

———

*The player has
to suggest:
1. For whom and in
what circumstances
the item on the card
would provide
positive values.
2. For whom and in
what circumstances
the item on the card
would provide
negative values.*

———

*It is never permitted to
say that the item
could be sold to
provide positive values.
This also applies to
renting out the item.
This game is best
played cooperatively,
with all players
making suggestions.
The game continues
with a new card.*

HOW DO I DESIGN THIS?

design

is a matter of *putting things together* to

ACHIEVE some OBJECTIVE.

The pictures show different buildings from around the world. The ingredients for the buildings are very similar. What makes the difference is the design.

THINKARD
GAME
**DESIGN
A STORY**

———

*The pack is shuffled
and four cards are
dealt face up to a
player. The player
may discard one of
the cards and then
start telling a story*

Usually there are a number of things that have to be kept in mind. In the case of a building, it must be good for its purpose (offices, residence, hospital, theater), it must look good and fit into the surroundings, it must comply with building and fire regulations, and it must be done within the available budget.

You can, of course, use a standard design or copy someone else's design, but design usually involves some element of creativity. A designer tries to do something new and original. You can design a new train. You can design a shoe. You can design a flag for a new country. You can design a pipe.

THINKARD
GAME
**DESIGN
A GAME**

———

*The task is to design a
new game using the
Thinkards. The game
should be a
"collection" game for
two people. Each
person is trying to*

PIPE

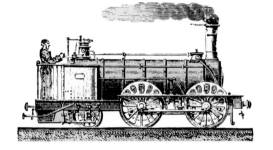

TRAIN

SHOE

*using the remaining
three cards. The story
may contain any
number of characters.
When the story has
been set up, two more
cards are dealt face
up to the player who
must continue the
story using either one
of the cards. The other
card can be discarded.
The game continues
either until the player
cannot continue or
until six cards have
been used in the story.*

*collect something.
What could that
something be? How do
the players get the
cards? Can disputes be
avoided? Be sure that
the game can actually
be played with the
available Thinkards.*

There are three things to be kept

in mind with any design:

1. What are you trying to ACHIEVE?

This is the "*objective.*"

2. What are the FACTORS or

CONSTRAINTS that you must consider?

3. What MATERIALS or

INGREDIENTS are available?

THINKARD
GAME

DESIGN A TOURIST ATTRACTION

Tourism is the biggest industry in the world. Tourism may involve traveling within your own country or going to another country.

You may travel because of the weather, in order to see the sights, or to take part in some sport or activity. The task is to design a ▶

THE PICTURES SHOW different designs of sails that have been used from time to time in different countries. All the sails are designed to make use of natural wind power.

The materials are not identical but are similar.
What sort of things would have influenced the design of these sails?

Pause and do your own thinking before reading further.

In most cases, the design of something evolves over a long period of time, with a series of small changes, rather than as a complete new design. In the above exercise, you might have considered the following factors: speed; maneuverability; sailing with or against the wind; ease of control; stability of the boat; the need to change speed; long-distance or near-shore use; cost.

▶ *tourist attraction. This should be a new type of tourist attraction rather than a traditional one.*

A player is dealt five cards face up. He or she must design a tourist attraction based on items in these five cards. If the player does not like these cards, then they are put aside and five new cards are dealt. If the player does not like these, then a final five cards are dealt. No more cards can be used. A design that uses all five cards is better than a design that only uses three. A design based on one card is not acceptable.

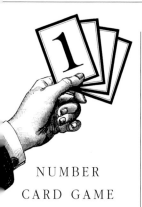

Design is much broader than just the VISUAL APPEARANCE of something.

So how do we judge which is the BEST?

NUMBER
CARD GAME
**DESIGN
A CROSS**

---

*Using any of the
number cards, how
many simple crosses
can you design? A
cross consists of three
cards in a column.
The middle card is
also the middle card
of a row of three
cards. So the cross
consists of a central
card with one card
above and one below.
Then there is one card
to the right and
another card to the left.*

---

*The object of the game
is to make the sum of
the three vertical cards
exactly the same as
the sum of the three
horizontal cards. For
example, the vertical
column might be
4 - 6 - 1 and the
horizontal row
might be 3 - 6 - 2.
Both column and
row add up to
the number 11.*

THINKARD
GAME
FUNCTIONS

---

*Look through the
Thinkards. See if you
can find an item
whose function could
be carried out
(perhaps not as well)
by a combination of
other cards. Two
players looking
through the cards can
compete to see
who can find the
most examples.*

THE PICTURES show three different bridges. Study each one carefully. Which one do you think is the best design?

By looking at the design, it is impossible to tell which is better. It would be necessary to know the span, the height of the banks, the amount of traffic going under and over the bridge, the cost, and numerous other factors.

problem solving

A problem is usually some difficulty or thing that we want to overcome or be rid of. The term "problem" can also be used when we are trying to achieve some task, though in many cases "design" or "task achieving" are more appropriate.

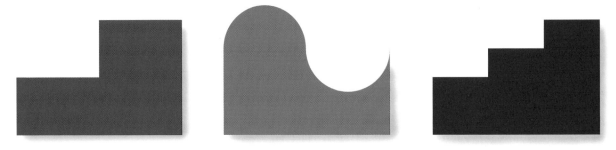

EACH OF THESE shapes can be divided into two equal halves so that each half could be fitted exactly over the other half. How could this be done? Check your answers on pages 70-71

When the course of action toward a desired objective is not easy or routine, then we say that we have a "problem."

The traditional method for problem solving is to find the cause of the problem and then to seek to remove that cause. If you feel a sharp pain when you sit on a particular chair, you would seek out the cause and then remove it. Finding

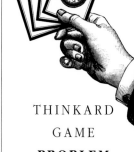

the cause may involve imagining some possible causes and then checking them out, one by one. If your television stops working, you could ask yourself, Is the problem in the television? Has the fuse blown? Is there a problem at the broadcasting station rather than with my television? With all problems we run through a list of possibilities before making a decision.

When auto accidents occur, we try to find out what the causes may have been: weather conditions, loss of control, drunk driving, brake failure, or falling asleep at the wheel.

We then try to solve these problems by introducing laws against speeding, by improving road signs, by inspecting vehicles more thoroughly, and by public awareness campaigns warning us of the dangers of drink driving.

Sometimes, there is no *simple*
"SOLUTION" to the PROBLEM.

In such cases, the cause cannot be eliminated, and other strategies must be adopted. We have alarms and protection against theft because we cannot remove the cause. We have buildings that are designed to resist earthquakes because we cannot prevent earthquakes from happening.

When we CANNOT SOLVE a problem
by removing the cause, then we have to
DESIGN A WAY FORWARD – even if the
CAUSE stays in place. We either act to
prevent or we *respond.*

Many of the items on the Thinkards can be seen as "solving" some problem. For example, an umbrella solves the problem of getting wet in the rain. A hose solves the problem of getting water to where it is needed without having to carry it.

Sometimes, the item allows us to do something that we could not do at all before. At other times, the item makes it simpler or more ▶

Every year throughout the world, people in developed countries produce an enormous amount of garbage. This is a problem that must be tackled in both these ways. We need to try to reduce the amount of garbage that is being and will be produced, but we also need to find ways of dealing with the garbage that has already been generated.

One of the key solutions to the garbage problem is recycling. Paper, glass bottles, and aluminum cans can all be recycled. Vegetable matter can be used as compost. Packaging material can be designed to be biodegradable. Perhaps packaging could have secondary uses. Are there any other ways to solve the problem of garbage?

▶ *convenient to do something that we could do before. So many of the items could be seen as "solutions" to a problem.*

In this game, the players work cooperatively. The top card of the pack is turned over. The players seek to identify the problem that the card solves and to describe this problem. They could then go on to say how this same problem might be tackled in a different way. If a particular card shows an item that does not seem to solve any problem, the players go on to the next card. In any case, the next card is turned over when the first card has been tackled.

WHICH HAT SHALL WE WEAR?

the six
thinking hats

In cultures with a tradition of ARGUMENT, one person *takes a position* on a subject and another person *attacks that position.*

So A attacks B and B attacks A. This method is used in law courts, in government, in business negotiations, and in family discussions. In some cases, it is quite useful, but it is not the only way to explore a subject. Some cultures find the method too aggressive. It can also seem that each side is more interested in winning the argument than in actually exploring the subject.

A hat is a piece of clothing that you put on and take off with ease. In many cultures, a hat is associated with the role that someone is playing at a particular moment. It is often associated with thinking: "Let's put on our thinking caps."

When we are thinking about something, we are usually

COMMENT

To play the Six Hats Game, please refer to pages 3-4 of the *Mind Games* leaflet.

trying to do everything at once. We might be looking for dangers and difficulties – why something will not work. We might be trying to find new ideas. We might be looking for more information. Then there are our feelings and emotions that try to interfere all the time. Can we separate out all these difficult types of thinking?

A golfer has many different clubs in his or her bag. One club is suitable for some situations; other situations require a different club. You could play golf using only one club. But you would be beaten by a player who used a full set.

Why do we ASSUME that there is ONE SETTING that will be adequate for all our thinking? *Why* do we try to do EVERYTHING AT ONCE?

The Six Thinking Hats method is now used worldwide in all kinds of organizations, ranging from major businesses to families and schools. It is used because it is simple and practical. When an issue is discussed, everyone present applies a particular hat to that issue and thinks in the same direction.

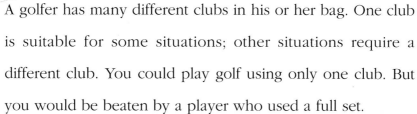

The six hats of different colors represent EVERY BASIC TYPE OF THINKING.

the white hat

White suggests paper. The white hat concerns information. When we wear the white hat, we ask the following kinds of questions: "What information do we have?"; "What information do we need?"; "What information is missing?"; "How are we going to get the information we need?"; "What questions should we be asking?" The white hat is used to direct attention to available or missing information.

the red hat

Red suggests fire and warmth. The red hat has to do with feelings, intuition, and emotions. You may not know the reasons why you like something, or why you do not like something. When the red hat is in use, you have the opportunity to describe your feelings and intuitions without any explanation at all. Your feelings exist, and the red hat gives you permission to vocalize these feelings.

the black hat

This is probably the most useful hat. It is certainly the hat that is most often used. Black reminds us of a judge's robes. The black hat is for caution. The black hat stops us from doing things that may be harmful. The black hat points out the risks and why something may not work. Without the black hat, we would be in trouble all the time. However, the black hat should not be overused, as overuse may be dangerous.

the green hat

Green suggests vegetation, which suggests growth, energy, and life. The green hat is the energy hat. Under the green hat, you offer proposals and suggestions and discuss new ideas and alternatives. Under the green hat, you talk about modifications and variations for a suggested idea. The green hat allows you to bring up possibilities. When the green hat is in use, everyone makes an effort to be creative.

the blue hat

The blue hat is for looking at the thinking process itself: "What should we do next?"; "What have we achieved so far?" We use the blue hat at the beginning of a discussion in order to define what we are thinking about and to decide what we want to have achieved at the end of our thinking. The blue hat may be used to order the sequence of hats that we are going to be using and to summarize what we have achieved.

the yellow hat

Yellow suggests sunshine and optimism. Under the yellow hat we make a direct effort to find the values and benefits in a suggestion: "What is good about this?" Even if we do not like the idea, the yellow hat asks us to seek out the good points. "Where are the benefits?"; "Who is going to benefit?"; "How will the benefits come about?"; "What are the different values?"

CONCLUSION

start again

At this point, you may have enjoyed parts of the book. Some of it may have been a little confusing. With time, things will become clearer and simpler as your thinking skills get better and better. Treat the book as a tennis court. Practice the different strokes on your own, or with a partner.

In time, you will know how to think. You will know how to watch yourself thinking. You will know how to watch others thinking. You will be in control of your own thinking. With repetition, the games will help you develop thinking as a skill.

At first, activities such as riding a bicycle and driving a car are difficult and not very enjoyable. But as your skill grows, so does your enjoyment and your sense of being in control. It is the same with thinking.

Once you have started to

enjoy thinking – KEEP GOING.

Read the book again and again.

Thinking need not be boring. Thinking need not be frightening. Thinking need not be intimidating. Thinking can be your hobby. The most important thing you can take from this book is that thinking is enjoyable.

answers

pp. 12–17 Recognition

p. 14 Of the four types of mushrooms, *A* and *C* are edible. *B* is *Amanita muscaria* (fly agaric), a poisonous mushroom whose toxins attack the central nervous system, producing effects such as hallucination, euphoria, hyperactivity, coma, and possible death. *D* is *Amantia phalloides* (death cap), a deadly poisonous mushroom that, even in very small amounts, causes diarrhea and vomiting, and although the victim appears to recover, the poison is still circulating in the bloodstream and causes fatal liver and kidney failure.

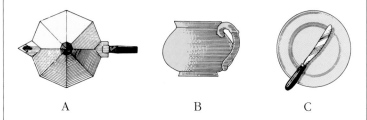

A   B   C

p. 15 The three objects shown in silhouettes are: *A* coffee pot; *B* pitcher; *C* plate and knife.

p. 15 Familiar faces: *A* Madonna; *B* Princess Diana; *C* Arnold Schwarzenegger; *D* Nelson Mandela. The face on the jigsaw puzzle is Albert Einstein.

A   B   C   D

p. 16 The painting is *The Circus* (1890–91) by the Pointillist painter, Georges-Pierre Seurat (1859–91).

p. 17 The flags represent: *A* Australia *B* Norway; *C* Belize; *D* Ireland; *E* Liberia; *F* India; *G* Iceland; *H* New Zealand.

pp. 18–21 Concepts

p. 18 Three possible pairing arrangements are: car and typewriter (mechanical extension devices); pencil and snake (long and thin); horse and hen (farm animals).

p. 21 There are two differences between the hot air balloon and the blimp. The blimp uses a gas that is always lighter than air (helium or hydrogen), while the hot air balloon heats up ordinary air. Secondly, the hot air balloon just follows air currents, while the blimp has engines to enable it to chart a course.

The plane and helicopter are different in the ways they achieve flight. The entire body of the plane must move through the air to achieve lift, whereas it is only the rotor blades of the helicopter that must move. This difference means that the helicopter can move directly upwards, downwards, and forwards; a plane can only move forwards.

The rocket is different from all of them because it does not "fly" through the air. The energy of the burning fuel lifts it off the ground, and momentum keeps it going when the fuel is gone.

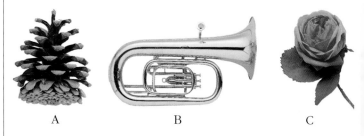

A   B   C

pp. 22–25 Possibilities

p. 22 The distorted objects are: *A* fir cone; *B* tuba; *C* rose.

p. 23 The shape that doesn't belong is *C*: it is the only non-equilateral shape.

p. 24 One way to balance the box on its edge is to attach a heavy weight with a vertical strip to the far side of the box. The weight hangs below the table and keeps the box upright on its edge.

p. 25 In the maze puzzle, the rule for the black route is as follows: if you meet a red square on your right, turn right after passing it and keep going straight until you come to the next red square; if you meet a red square on your left, turn left after passing the red square and keep going until you come to the next red square. The rule for the red route is as follows: if you meet a blue followed by a green on either side, turn right after passing them; if you meet a green followed by a blue on either side, turn left after passing them. Otherwise keep going straight.

pp. 26–29 Judgment

p. 27 The lines that are equal in length to A are: B, C, E, H, I, and L.

p. 28 The four countries are: A Australia; B China; C United States; D Brazil.

p. 28 All four squares have exactly the same number of dots: 20.

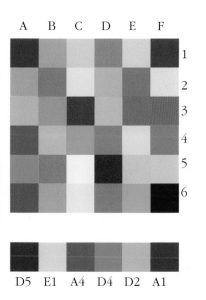

A B C D E F
1
2
3
4
5
6

D5 E1 A4 D4 D2 A1

p. 29 The matching tints are: D5, E1, A4, D4, D2, and A1.

pp 30-35 Alternatives

p. 32 There are 28 routes through the maze from A to B: EGHJ; EGJH; ECDF; ECFD; ECFH; EFHJ; EFCD; EGHF; EGIJ; GEFH; GJHF; GIJH; GECD; GECF; GEFD; GHFD; CDFH; CEFH; CEGH; CEGJ; CEFD; CFHJ; IJHF; IGHF; IJGH; IGEF; IGHJ; IGJH.

p. 34 The alternative methods that can be used to attach one piece of wood to another include the following: nails; screws; binding; glue; staples; dowels; bolts and nuts; plates and brackets; rivets and washers.

pp. 36–41 Comparison & Choice

p. 38 Both of the flowers shown in the illustration are popular types of chrysanthemum.

pp. 42–45 Analysis

p. 42 The four pieces that have been used to form the square are: A, C, E, and F.

p. 43 The item of furniture that is made from the various pieces of wood is a chair.

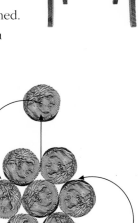

pp. 46–51 Perception

p. 48 The task is much easier if you look at the triangle of coins as a rosette with three extra coins attached. All you need to do is to move each coin around to the next position and the triangle now points downward.

p. 49 You may have decided to count the filled-in circles. Or you may see it as an arrangement of 6 x 6 = 36 circles. You count up the empty circles and subtract the total from 36.

p. 50 There are 14 squares in the grid.

pp. 52–55 Values & Feelings

p. 55 The following are suggestions for the four expressions: A puzzled, concerned, tense, etc. B happy, relaxed, C quizzical, bemused; D seductive, thoughtful, contemplative.

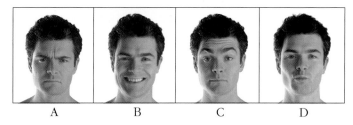

A   B   C   D

pp. 60–63 Values & Feelings

p. 60 The shapes can be divided in exact halves as shown.

acknowledgments

PICTURE ACKNOWLEDGMENTS
Key: t=top; b=bottom; c=centre; l=left; r=right; a=above

Dorling Kindersley would like to thank the following for their kind permission to reproduce the photographs:

Hulton-Deutsch Collection
p.11 bl, p.15 bc

Courtesy of IKEA Ltd.
p.54 ca, cra, cb, c, crb

Magnum Photos Ltd.
Philip J. Griffiths p.53 t

MIRA
p.61 t

Musée de Louvre, Paris
p.10 (detail), p.51 *The Marriage At Cana* by Veronese

Musée d'Orsay, Paris
p.11 (detail), p.16 *The Circus* by Seurat

National Motor Museum, Beaulieu
p.40 bl, bc

Panos Pictures
Marc Schlossman p.63 c

Retna Pictures Ltd.
Steve Granitz p.15 clb, p.70 cl; Michael Melia p.15 bl, p.70 cl; Clemens Rikken p.15 br, p.70 cl; Rocky Widner p.15 crb, p.70 cl

Rex Features Ltd.
Sipa Press p.62 t; p.64 c

Royal Horticultural Society
p.38 tl

Science Photo Library
Scott Camazine p.8 cr; Custom Medical Stock Photo p.7

Tony Stone Images
Ken Biggs p.44 c

Studio Editions Ltd.
p.20 c, p.64 clb, bl, tr, p.65 tl, p.71

SPECIAL PHOTOGRAPHY
Jane Burton p.40; Andy Crawford p.39 r; Neil Fletcher p.14 b; Steve Gorton p.40 cl; Frank Greenaway pp.38-39; Marc Henrie p.26 t; Dave King p.38 b, p.40 bl, bc, pp.40-41, p.55; Cyril Laubscher p. 37, p.39 l; Tracy Morgan pp.26-27, p.40 c; David Murray p.31 cl; David and Michael Murray p. 54 tl; Stephen Oliver p.56 cr; Tim Ridley pp.10 br-11 b; Matthew Ward p.59 c; Jerry Young p. 40 tr

ILLUSTRATIONS
Karen Cochrane p.20 crb (hovercraft), p.21 tl, tr (helicopter, rocket)
Vanessa Lough p.49 b
Mandy Pritty p.2, p.12, p.30, p.36, p.46, p.69
Mark Davies p.13, p.24, pp.34-35, p.48 br, p.70 br
Phil Ormerod p.23, p.25, p.28 b, pp.32-33, p.42, pp.48 t-49 t, p.60
Zirrinia Austin p.29

Dorling Kindersley would like to thank Paddy Hills, Dr. de Bono's assistant, whose helpfulness made this book possible; Dover Publications Inc, New York, for permission to include several Dover images in the book; Kirstie Hills for editorial assistance; Darren Hill for design assistance.

For more information about Dr. de Bono's
- Public seminars
- Private seminars
- Certified Training Programs
- Thinking programs for schools
- CD-ROM
- Books and tapes
- CoRT Thinking Lessons

Please call or write:
Diane McQuaig
The McQuaig Group
132 Rochester Ave.
Toronto, Ontario
Canada, M4N 1P1

Tel: (416) 488-0008 Fax: (416) 488-4544